A LIFEGUIDE® BIBLE STUDY

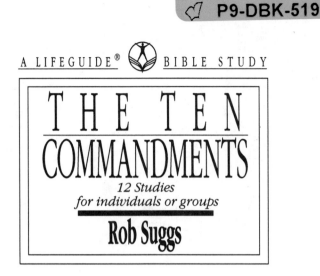

THE TEN
COMMANDMENTS

*12 Studies
for individuals or groups*

Rob Suggs

With Notes for Leaders

InterVarsity Press
Downers Grove, Illinois

InterVarsity Press® is the book-publishing division of InterVarsity Christian Fellowship®, a student movement active on campus at hundreds of universities, colleges and schools of nursing in the United States of America, and a member movement of the International Fellowship of Evangelical Students. For information about local and regional activities, write Public Relations Dept., InterVarsity Christian Fellowship, 6400 Schroeder Rd., P.O. Box 7895, Madison, WI 53707-7895.

Cover photograph: Dennis Flaherty

ISBN 0-8308-1084-6

Printed in the United States of America ∞

| 21 | 20 | 19 | 18 | 17 | 16 | 15 | 14 | 13 | 12 | 11 | 10 | 9 | 8 | 7 | 6 | 5 | 4 | 3 |
| 15 | 14 | 13 | 12 | 11 | 10 | 09 | 08 | 07 | 06 | 05 | 04 | 03 | 02 | 01 | 00 | | | |

Contents

Getting the Most
from LifeGuide® Bible Studies

Many of us long to fill our minds and our lives with Scripture. We desire to be transformed by its message. LifeGuide® Bible Studies are designed to be an exciting and challenging way to do just that. They help us to be guided by God's Word in every area of life.

How They Work

LifeGuides have a number of distinctive features. Perhaps the most important is that they are *inductive* rather than *deductive*. In other words, they lead us to *discover* what the Bible says rather than simply *telling* us what it says.

They are also thought-provoking. They help us to think about the meaning of the passage so that we can truly understand what the author is saying. The questions require more than one-word answers.

The studies are personal. Questions expose us to the promises, assurances, exhortations and challenges of God's Word. They are designed to allow the Scriptures to renew our minds so that we can be transformed by the Spirit of God. This is the ultimate goal of all Bible study.

The studies are versatile. They are designed for student, neighborhood and church groups. They are also effective for individual study.

How They're Put Together

LifeGuides also have a distinctive format. Each study need take no more than forty-five minutes in a group setting or thirty minutes in personal study—unless you choose to take more time.

The studies can be used within a quarter system in a church and fit well in a semester or trimester system on a college campus. If a guide has more than thirteen studies, it is divided into two or occasionally three parts of approximately twelve studies each.

LifeGuides use a workbook format. Space is provided for writing answers to each question. This is ideal for personal study and allows group members to prepare in advance for the discussion.

The studies also contain leader's notes. They show how to lead a group discussion, provide additional background information on certain questions, give helpful tips on group dynamics and suggest ways to deal with problems which may arise during the discussion. With such helps, someone with little or no experience can lead an effective study.

Suggestions for Individual Study

1. As you begin each study, pray that God will help you to understand and apply the passage to your life.

2. Read and reread the assigned Bible passage to familiarize yourself with what the author is saying. In the case of book studies, you may want to read through the entire book prior to the first study. This will give you a helpful overview of its contents.

3. A good modern translation of the Bible, rather than the King James Version or a paraphrase, will give you the most help. The New International Version, the New American Standard Bible and the Revised Standard Version are all recommended. However, the questions in this guide are based on the New International Version.

4. Write your answers in the space provided in the study guide. This will help you to express your understanding of the passage clearly.

5. It might be good to have a Bible dictionary handy. Use it to look up any unfamiliar words, names or places.

Suggestions for Group Study

1. Come to the study prepared. Follow the suggestions for individual

study mentioned above. You will find that careful preparation will greatly enrich your time spent in group discussion.

2. Be willing to participate in the discussion. The leader of your group will not be lecturing. Instead, he or she will be encouraging the members of the group to discuss what they have learned from the passage. The leader will be asking the questions that are found in this guide. Plan to share what God has taught you in your individual study.

3. Stick to the passage being studied. Your answers should be based on the verses which are the focus of the discussion and not on outside authorities such as commentaries or speakers. This guide deliberately avoids jumping from book to book or passage to passage. Each study focuses on only one passage. Book studies are generally designed to lead you through the book in the order in which it was written. This will help you follow the author's argument.

4. Be sensitive to the other members of the group. Listen attentively when they share what they have learned. You may be surprised by their insights! Link what you say to the comments of others so the group stays on the topic. Also, be affirming whenever you can. This will encourage some of the more hesitant members of the group to participate.

5. Be careful not to dominate the discussion. We are sometimes so eager to share what we have learned that we leave too little opportunity for others to respond. By all means participate! But allow others to also.

6. Expect God to teach you through the passage being discussed and through the other members of the group. Pray that you will have an enjoyable and profitable time together.

7. If you are the discussion leader, you will find additional suggestions and helpful ideas for each study in the leader's notes. These are found at the back of the guide.

Introducing the Ten Commandments

Bill Watterson's comic strip character, Calvin, challenges Hobbes the tiger to an outdoor game. He hits a grounder, only to finds Hobbes has beaten him to first base. Undaunted, the boy turns and sprints for third, or he quickly creates a new base. Maybe he punts. All's fair in "Calvinball," a chaotic competition in which rules are spontaneous and unbinding.

Watterson has retired his comic strip. But here in the real world, many of us are playing out our own versions of "Calvinball." Rules are recognized and affirmed—until they become inconvenient. What absolute principles govern business endeavors? Is marriage really "'til death do us part?" After a few rounds of the game, we begin to wonder if rules are such a bad thing after all. We begin to yearn for simple, value-enriched guidelines for living. The problem: Who writes the rules and marks the boundaries?

Thousands of years ago, the people of God found themselves at a similar crossroad in the wilderness. Behind them lay slavery and degradation, ahead gleamed the promise of freedom and prosperity. All things seemed possible—including loss of direction, starvation and exposure. Some of them began to have second thoughts about this freedom idea. After all, slavery had its points: security, for one. Freedom, once acquired, can be terrifying.

At this defining moment, Moses climbed a mountain to seek the answers from the God who had provided the freedom. When he descended, he carried in his hands and heart a concise declaration of wisdom for the ages. We know it as The Ten Commandments, though the Old Testament speaks of the "Ten Words."

Are these the boundaries we crave? Yes, but they are much more than that. These are rules that restrict, yet give freedom. They are words of prevention, but also protection. They are both fundamental and profound, inner-directed and outward-reaching. God gave us ten words that establish identity: ours and his. The Ten Commandments constitute a "Declaration of Dependence." They affirm our dependence on God and each other.

Several years ago, a well-known media magnate issued his own update of the commandments. The old, "negative" ones, he declared, had become so much religious baggage. He offered the world an alternative list of ten politically correct "affirmations" to replace the dreary old commandments. More recently, Cullen Murphy in *The Atlantic Monthly* observed that, "Suggestions for replacing the Ten Commandments altogether are, in fact, becoming common" ("Broken Covenant?" November 1996, pp. 22-24). Not too surprisingly, these updates fail to catch on. It turns out that people are drawn to those dusty words engraved on the courthouse door. They are willing to affirm that such acts as killing and stealing are, yes, "negative."

The commandments retain their power. As a matter of fact, you might be surprised by their everyday relevance. The stones on which God's finger etched the commandments are lost, but the words live on; for our own hearts bear his fingerprints. And we understand that these laws point to deeper truths. Ten words mark the starting point to knowing God and living in society; but they lead us to yet another crossroad, where law ends and grace begins.

On the way, however, there is a mountain to climb. Alongside Moses, we seek God's face, and our prayer is to receive the Word of Life clearly and eagerly. Like Moses, we will come away from the encounter with glowing faces, and people will know at a glance that we have encountered not just God's laws, but God himself.

1
Laying Down the Law
Exodus 20

It's tough being a child. At every turn there are new laws: the Law of Crossing the Street, the Law of Speaking and Interrupting. Then there is the complex maze of the Dinner Table Law. Childhood is marked by the hearing and internalizing of instruction. If we accept and follow these customs, we become capable, functioning adults.

The book of Exodus describes the childhood of Israel. A loving father delivers the law to his children; it is encapsulated in the Ten Commandments.

---

1. When and how did your parents first give you "freedom" as a teen or young adult?

---

2. Read Exodus 20. What stands out as you hear the law delivered?

3. What is important about the context of the commandments, as set by God in verse 2?

---

4. The first four commands (vv. 3-11) focus on God. Why should they come first?

---

5. In your opinion what is the unifying theme of these commands about God?

---

6. The final six laws concern human relationships. What would you describe as the theme of these verses?

---

7. What logic do you find in the order of the final five commandments in verses 13-17?

---

8. The Israelites fall back in fear from the manifestations of God's presence (vv. 18-19). To what extent is fear a positive reaction to the laws of God?

9. How exactly is God testing the Israelites (v. 20)?

10. Given what the people have experienced, why is a sacrifice appropriate (v. 24)?

11. Which commandment presents the greatest challenge to you?

12. In what one way can you be more obedient to God in the coming week?

In what one way you can be more loving to others?

2
The One and Only

1 Kings 18:16-39

Welcome to the age of the guru! Choose among a wide assortment of health gurus, fitness gurus, investment gurus, technology gurus, self-help gurus and, presumably, gurus of guruism. But sometimes gurus collide: Which has the best diet plan or career-path strategy? It's your call.

Thankfully, the first commandment simplifies things. It's message is this: Follow the Leader—the only Leader.

---

1. Almost anything can be a "god." From your observation, what "gods" or pursuits are the most popular today?

---

2. Exodus 20:3 says, "You shall have no other gods before me." What are the implications of placing this commandment first?

3. Read 1 Kings 18:16-39. Elijah, God's prophet, is confronting King Ahab during a drought. What does Ahab's epithet—"you troubler of Israel"—reveal about his conscience (v. 17)?

---

4. What are the risks Elijah takes by calling for a public confrontation (v. 19)?

---

5. Mt. Carmel was a location commonly used for the worship of Baal. Why should we challenge competing gods "on their own turf"?

What are some possible contexts ("turfs") in which the gods of this world can be confronted and challenged today?

---

6. The Hebrew term used for *waver* can also mean "to limp." What is the significance of the accusation Elijah makes of the people (v. 21)?

7. Elijah employs historic symbolism in building his altar (v. 31). Why is this important?

8. Water would be a precious commodity during a drought. Why would Elijah make a show of pouring it repeatedly over an altar built for fire (vv. 33-34)?

9. In verse 37 Elijah pleads for God to turn the people's hearts back to him. Why do people turn away from God?

10. What concerns or pursuits in your own life threaten to come before your complete devotion to the Lord?

3
Idol Minds

Exodus 32

Vince finally owns it: the ultimate automobile. Ever since he spotted that certain make and model three years ago, he has been obsessed with making one his own—despite a modest income. After long, tiring months and a second job, the down-payment became a reality. Vince is so proud and protective he is almost afraid to take the car out in traffic. He loves to wash it, wax it and sit behind the wheel just to hear the wonderful sound of the car idling—or is that idoling?

---

1. Describe an acquisition you once desired more than anything in the world and what happened when you got it

---

2. Exodus 20:4-6 says:

You shall not make for yourself an idol in the form of anything in heaven above or on the earth beneath or in the waters below. You shall not bow down to them or worship them; for I, the LORD your

God, am a jealous God, punishing the children for the sin of the fathers to the third and fourth generation of those who hate me, but showing love to a thousand generations of those who love me and keep my commandments.

What is the difference between the first commandment ("no other gods before me") and the second?

3. What are the characteristics of an idol, according to these verses?

4. Explain what is meant by a "jealous" God (v. 5).

5. Why might this sin (as well as its avoidance) affect future generations (vv. 5-6)?

6. Read Exodus 32. These events occur while Moses is on the mountain receiving the law. What seems to cause the Israelites to yearn for new gods?

7. What is the significance of the material out of which the people cast their idols (vv. 2-4)?

8. What is the relationship between idols and "revelry" (v. 6, see also v. 25)?

9. Moses is concerned that the people have become "a laughingstock to their enemies" (v. 25). What messages do believers send through idol worship and its consequences?

10. The consequences of Israelite unfaithfulness are severe (vv. 27-29), in keeping with the detailed warning of the commandment (20:4-6). Why do you think this particular violation so offends God?

11. What potential "golden calves" threaten to steal Christians' allegiance today?

12. Moses immediately melted the golden calf. What idols need to be confronted in your own life?

4
Respect for the Name
Psalm 96

Once there was a young, shy boy from Chicago who wanted to be a cartoonist. He managed to create the first "talking" cartoon short, "Steamboat Willie," from which a star emerged: Mickey Mouse. But when you hear the name Walt Disney today, you probably don't think of the man who died in 1966. You think of a certain standard of film. You think of an entertainment empire. The name has outlived its owner and taken on a life of its own. The third commandment is based on the power of a name.

1. What do you know about the history and meaning of your name?

2. Exodus 20:7 says, "You shall not misuse the name of the LORD your God, for the LORD will not hold anyone guiltless who misuses his name." Explain the meaning of this commandment.

3. What is the difference, if any, between this commandment and profanity?

4. How does the third commandment build on the first two?

5. Read Psalm 96. What is the theme of this psalm?

6. Why is it good to sing "a new song" to the Lord (v. 1)?

7. Why would we praise God's name, as opposed to simply praising God (v. 2)?

8. Verse 3 deals with declaring his glory to the nations. How should the issues of evangelism and missions influence us in the proper use of God's name?

9. How can we ascribe to God (and thus his name) glory and strength (v. 7)?

10. How does making an offering give glory to God's name (v. 8)?

11. Verses 10-13 deal with the natural world. How does nature contribute to our use of God's name?

12. Spend a period of time reflecting on the glory of God's name and make a commitment to declare his glory in the coming week.

5
Respect for Sabbath Rest
Psalm 16

Eric Liddell had waited his whole life to run one race. But, as the world watched in shock, he withdrew his name. The Olympic organizers had scheduled the qualifying heat on a Sunday, and as a Christian Liddell felt he would be dishonoring God by participating. As the movie *Chariots of Fire* tells us, he managed to win the gold medal in another race entirely.

Would you have done the same? Few of us hold the Sabbath in such regard today. What is the Sabbath all about? The fourth commandment offers answers.

---

1. What was a typical Sunday afternoon like in the home in which you were raised?

---

2. Read Exodus 20:8-11:

Remember the Sabbath day by keeping it holy. Six days you shall

labor and do all your work, but the seventh day is a Sabbath to the
LORD your God. On it you shall not do any work, neither you, nor
your son or daughter, nor your manservant or maidservant, nor
your animals, nor the alien within your gates. For in six days the
LORD made the heavens and the earth, the sea, and all that is in
them, but he rested on the seventh day. Therefore the LORD blessed
the Sabbath day and made it holy.

What does the explanation for this commandment imply about the
relationship between God and humanity (v. 11)?

3. What do you think is meant by "keeping it holy"?

4. Read Psalm 16, David's song of rest. What are some sources of
delight for the psalmist (vv. 2-7)?

5. What observations help David find peace with his "lot in life" (vv.
5-6)?

6. How do God's presence and teaching affect the psalmist (vv. 7-8)?

7. What are some good ways to find rest in "practicing the presence of God"?

8. How does David face the uncertainty of the future (vv. 9-10)?

9. Given this psalm, how would you summarize David's approach to rest?

10. What issues in life currently keep you from rest?

11. What arrangements can you make to better keep the Sabbath holy and find personal rest?

12. Pray that you would "set the Lord always before [you]" this week, that your "body also will rest secure."

6
Respect for Parents
Ruth 1:1-18

The Sandwich Generation: we're not talking diets, but demographics. Young adults are starting their own families later in life, while their own parents have greater life expectancies. The result? This group finds itself "sandwiched" between caring for the two adjacent generations—their aging parents and their children—simultaneously. They are not to envied.

Or are they? The Bible consistently teaches veneration of the elderly. In particular, we are blessed when we honor our parents.

---

1. What was the best gift your parents ever gave you?

---

2. Exodus 20:12 says, "Honor your father and your mother, so that you may live long in the land the LORD your God is giving you." The final six commandments govern human relationships. Why do you think this particular one would be found at the top of them?

---

3. Paul calls this "the first commandment with a promise—'that it may go well with you and that you may enjoy long life on the earth' " (Eph 6:2-3). Does this commandment in fact promise long life for those who respect their parents? Explain.

---

4. Read Ruth 1:1-18. While Naomi and Ruth are not related by birth, what factors would contribute to their acting as parent and child?

---

5. For what reasons would Naomi dismiss her daughters-in-law and choose to travel alone (vv. 8-9)?

---

6. Describe Naomi's spiritual outlook (v. 13).

Do you feel this outlook is motivated more by unselfishness or bitterness? Why?

7. What sacrifices does Ruth make in her commitment to stay with Naomi (vv. 16-17)?

8. Ruth's commitment extends to death and burial. How is it beneficial to verbalize such a commitment to our parents?

9. As the story plays out, Ruth marries (and finds a place in the birth line of Jesus); Naomi becomes a "grandmother." What are the rewards of being faithful to our parents?

10. In your opinion, how does our culture view the elderly?

11. If your parents are living, what are three ways you can express your love and commitment to them? (If your parents aren't living, then think of some other elderly relative or friend.)

7
Respect for Life
1 Samuel 24

Wall-to-wall violence, an exponential body count, nonstop mayhem—and that's just Saturday morning television.

Our culture is fascinated by death; and features it, of all places, in its entertainment. Today's children are raised on video games in which they roam virtual corridors with virtual assault weapons, blowing away hordes of enemies, until killing becomes casual. Harmless play? That's a question for behavioral science. But the sixth commandment is plain and simple: "You shall not murder." As we will see, the Scriptures teach us to choose life.

---

1. Why do you think people find the subject of murder (in novels, movies and news items, for instance) so intriguing?

---

2. Exodus 20:13 says, "You shall not murder." The Hebrew version of verses 13-15 contains only six words—the equivalent of "No murder.

No adultery. No stealing." What is the general effect of this terseness?

_____

3. Read 1 Samuel 24. In this vivid narrative, Israel's King Saul is insecure about the growing fame of David—which he sees as a threat to his grip on the throne. How do Saul's "friends" encourage him to kill David (v. 4)?

_____

4. David clearly has an opportunity to kill the king (v. 4). How might he have rationalized this act?

_____

5. What do David's pangs of conscience reveal about his perspective (vv. 5-7)?

_____

6. What strategies does David use as a peacemaker (vv. 8-13)?

_____

7. What is the relationship between humility and respect for life?

8. Compare David's use of "spiritual reasoning" (v. 10) with that of Saul's men (v. 4).

9. How does David cast Saul's ethical and spiritual decision (vv. 14-15)?

10. What new insight does Saul verbalize regarding the cyclical nature of killing and vengeance (vv. 16-21)?

11. How have David and Saul affected their future prospects?

12. How can you personally take a stand for the biblical value of life?

8
Respect for Marriage
2 Samuel 11

T he book *Sex in America* reports that twenty percent of all women and as many as thirty-five percent of all men have been unfaithful in marriage. *Christianity Today* surveyed its readers and discovered that twenty-three percent of their subscribers admitted to having had affairs. *Leadership Journal* found that ten percent of the pastors and church leaders they surveyed had committed adultery. Can something so common be so wrong? The seventh commandment says yes, it can.

1. What factors do you think contribute to widespread adultery in our times?

2. Exodus 20:14 says, "You shall not commit adultery." What does adultery have in common with previous commandments?

3. Read 2 Samuel 11, which recounts the story of David's tragic liaison with Bathsheba. What is the true beginning of the king's ill-chosen course of action?

---

4. What do David's actions after he discovers Bathsheba's pregnancy reveal about him (vv. 6-9)?

---

5. Contrast Uriah's character and perspective with that of David (vv. 10-13).

---

6. Given the way the situation unfolds through verse 13, what factors do you think contribute to David's decision to commit murder (vv. 14-15)?

---

7. How does David's sin "ripple" outward to encourage sin in others (vv. 18-21)?

---

8. How have you seen this ripple effect of sin at work?

9. What evidence of David's remorse, or lack of it, can we find in the aftermath (vv. 15-17)?

Given that we know David was generally righteous and even "a man after God's heart" (1 Sam 13:14), how do you account for his lack of a guilty conscience?

10. Which of The Ten Commandments has David violated in the course of this chapter?

11. What lessons can we learn about adultery (and sin in general) from David's story?

12. What "temptation traps" in your life need to be neutralized to avoid the destructive spiral of sin?

13. Ask God to strengthen you in avoiding temptation and to help you stay away from those likely places where temptation is found.

9
Respect for Property
Acts 4:32—5:11

J an is happily pecking away at the keyboard. Armed with brand new financial software, she finds great satisfaction in computing her income, paying her bills and anticipating her expenses. One *non*-expense was the software because a friend let Jan copy his floppy disks. So this program was free, and Jan calls that good money management!

But the software manufacturer might call it something else. Jan knows that. *Surely* they expect a certain amount of "bootlegging," right? Don't they figure all that into their budgets? Could the eighth commandment have anything to do with computer software?

---

1. Describe an incident when you were the victim of theft.

---

2. Exodus 20:15 says, "You shall not steal." How many varieties of stealing can you name?

3. Read Acts 4:32—5:11. The setting is the first generation of Christianity. What is the relationship between unity and possessions (4:32)?

4. What is the relationship between sharing possessions and sharing the gospel (4:33)?

5. Describe the impact the believers had on their local economy (4:34-35).

How could the church today follow such a model?

6. Does this passage negate the concept of personal ownership for Christians? Explain.

7. What other sin, or sins, are involved in Ananias and Sapphira's actions (5:1-2)?

8. How does Peter show Ananias his sin in a different perspective (5:3-4)?

9. Ananias and Sapphira actually die as judgment for their sin (5:5-11). Why might the punishment be so severe in this particular context?

10. What are some ways Christians might steal from the church today?

11. What lessons relating to possessions should we learn from the early church?

12. How does God want you to make better use of your own possessions?

10
Respect for the Truth
Proverbs 12

W hat's so funny?" Dad asks his giggling children.

"We're trying to find out which of us has told the biggest whopper."

"When I was a kid, I never even *thought* about telling a lie," Dad replies.

The children whisper, then one speaks up. "I guess that's it; Dad's the winner!"

In our world, it might be said, honesty is more remarkable than lies. We're accustomed to "whoppers" in advertising, politics and polite society. We make jokes about the lies of lawyers and car dealers. We expect dishonesty from everyone. The ninth commandment speaks to the issue of truth-telling.

---

1. Describe an occasion (perhaps as a child or teenager) when you were caught in a lie.

2. Of all sins, lying is the one most identified with the devil ("father of lies," Jn 8:44). Why do you think this is so?

3. Exodus 20:16 says, "You shall not give false testimony against your neighbor." Compare lying, in its nature and consequences, to some of the other commandments.

4. Proverbs 12 repeatedly deals with the subject of honesty. Read Proverbs 12:5-7. What is the main theme of these three sayings?

5. How can honest words rescue someone (v. 6)?

6. Read Proverbs 12:13-14. What kinds of "traps" can wicked words set for us (v. 13)?

7. How can mere words fill us with good things (v. 14)?

What does "the work of (our) hands" have to do with this principle?

_____

8. Read Proverbs 12:17-23. The writer intermingles sayings about lying and reckless speech. What do they have in common?

Is it possible for someone to be reckless by being honest? Explain.

_____

9. What kinds of reckless speech are tempting to you?

_____

10. What point about honesty and lying is made by verse 19?

_____

11. How can God's response affect our honesty (v. 22)?

_____

12. Ask God to search your heart and examine your personal integrity. How can you use words to promote truth and peace this week?

11
The Value of Contentment
1 Timothy 6:3-10

And so we come to the last word, the grand finale: *You shall not covet.*

That's it? Somehow this command seems out of place. Does coveting even belong on the same list with idolatry, murder, theft and adultery? After all, it is simply a "thought crime." It inflicts no damage on others. Or does it?

The tenth and final commandment, moving from action to thought, suggests new possibilities. It foreshadows a new law, one which will concern itself less with the hands than with the heart.

---

1. What is the difference between coveting and innocent desire?

---

2. Exodus 20:17 says: "You shall not covet your neighbor's house. You shall not covet your neighbor's wife, or his manservant or maidservant, his ox or donkey, or anything that belongs to your neighbor." We have previously considered the order of the commandments. Why do you think this one falls last?

3. In your opinion why does God include specific examples in this particular commandment?

4. Read 1 Timothy 6:3-10. What is the nature of the controversy Paul describes (vv. 3-5)?

5. Given that the Proverbs teach that godly people often find material success, what is Paul upset about (v. 5)?

6. How does Paul use irony to underscore his point (vv. 5-6)?

7. How would you define "godliness with contentment" (v. 6)?

8. Does being content with food and clothing rule out other desires (v. 7)? Explain.

---

9. Give a description of Paul's "trap" and its workings (v. 9).

---

10. Verse 10 is often misquoted as "Money is the root of all evil." What difference does the true reading make in our understanding of money and ambition?

---

11. Which of the other commandments might coveting lead one to violate? Why?

---

12. How can you more actively strive toward godliness with contentment in your present situation?

12
The Law of Grace
Romans 3:9-31

God's commandments are as relevant today as ever. We affirm that out of our struggles as we seek to walk in obedience, we stumble and fall daily.

Jesus said that he came to fulfill, not abolish, the law. But his fulfillment of it carries us into a new relationship with the lawgiver: one that acknowledges the inevitability of our stumbling, and finds a new way to lift us up, dust us off, and restore us once and for all. Through Christ, we discover the law of grace.

1. When have you felt that your best efforts weren't good enough?

2. Read Romans 3:9-31. Paul is discussing the relationship of Jews and Gentiles to God. Considering that Paul was trained as a Pharisee (a Jewish religious leader specially concerned about purity through the law), what do you find most interesting or surprising here?

3. Paul quotes from a variety of Old Testament passages in verses 10-18. Describe the picture of humanity that he assembles.

Which of the Ten Commandments have been violated?

4. The Jews are "under sin" (v. 9) and "under the law" (v. 19). Why is this so?

5. How does the law make us conscious of sin (v. 20)?

6. Explain the significance of each of these terms from verses 21-24: righteousness, justification, grace and redemption.

7. For what purpose was Christ allowed to die (vv. 24-25)?

_____

8. How are God's grace and justice related?

_____

9. What is Paul's point in bringing up boasting (v. 27)?

_____

10. Why is the law not nullified by God's grace (v. 31)?

_____

11. Given what we have learned about grace, how should we relate to the commandments?

_____

12. What active response will you make to the loving grace of God?

Leader's Notes

Leading a Bible discussion can be an enjoyable and rewarding experience. But it can also be *scary*—especially if you've never done it before. If this is your feeling, you're in good company. When God asked Moses to lead the Israelites out of Egypt, he replied, "O Lord, please send someone else to do it!" (Ex 4:13).

When Solomon became king of Israel, he felt the task was beyond his abilities. "I am only a little child and do not know how to carry out my duties. . . . Who is able to govern this great people of yours?" (1 Kings 3:7, 9).

When God called Jeremiah to be a prophet, he replied, "Ah, Sovereign LORD, . . . I do not know how to speak; I am only a child" (Jer 1:6).

The list goes on. The apostles were "unschooled, ordinary men" (Acts 4:13). Timothy was young, frail and frightened. Paul's "thorn in the flesh" made him feel weak. But God's response to all of his servants—including you—is essentially the same: "My grace is sufficient for you" (2 Cor 12:9). Relax. God helped these people in spite of their weaknesses, and he can help you in spite of your feelings of inadequacy.

There is another reason why you should feel encouraged. Leading a Bible discussion is not difficult if you follow certain guidelines. You don't need to be an expert on the Bible or a trained teacher. The suggestions listed below should enable you to effectively and enjoyably fulfill your role as leader.

Preparing to Lead

1. Ask God to help you understand and apply the passage to your own life. Unless this happens, you will not be prepared to lead others. Pray too for the various members of the group. Ask God to give you an enjoyable and profitable time together studying his Word.

2. As you begin each study, read and reread the assigned Bible passage to familiarize yourself with what the author is saying. In the case of book studies, you may want to read through the entire book prior to the first study. This will give you a helpful overview of its contents.

3. This study guide is based on the New International Version of the Bible. It will help you and the group if you use this translation as the basis for your study and discussion. Encourage others to use the NIV also, but allow them the freedom to use whatever translation they prefer.

4. Carefully work through each question in the study. Spend time in meditation and reflection as you formulate your answers.

5. Write your answers in the space provided in the study guide. This will help you to express your understanding of the passage clearly.

6. It might help you to have a Bible dictionary handy. Use it to look up any unfamiliar words, names or places. (For additional help on how to study a passage, see chapter five of *Leading Bible Discussions,* IVP.)

7. Once you have finished your own study of the passage, familiarize yourself with the leader's notes for the study you are leading. These are designed to help you in several ways. First, they tell you the purpose the study guide author had in mind while writing the study. Take time to think through how the study questions work together to accomplish that purpose. Second, the notes provide you with additional background information or comments on some of the questions. This information can be useful if people have difficulty understanding or answering a question. Third, the leader's notes can alert you to potential problems you may encounter during the study.

8. If you wish to remind yourself of anything mentioned in the leader's notes, make a note to yourself below that question in the study.

Leading the Study

1. Begin the study on time. Unless you are leading an evangelistic Bible study, open with prayer, asking God to help you to understand and apply the passage.

2. Be sure that everyone in your group has a study guide. Encourage them to prepare beforehand for each discussion by working through the questions in the guide.

3. At the beginning of your first time together, explain that these studies are meant to be discussions not lectures. Encourage the members of the group to participate. However, do not put pressure on those who may be hesitant to speak during the first few sessions.

4. Read the introductory paragraph at the beginning of the discussion. This will orient the group to the passage being studied.

5. Read the passage aloud if you are studying one chapter or less. You may choose to do this yourself, or someone else may read if he or she has been asked to do so prior to the study. Longer passages may occasionally be read in parts at different times during the study. Some studies may cover several chapters. In such cases reading aloud would probably take too much time, so the group members should simply read the assigned passages prior to the study.

6. As you begin to ask the questions in the guide, keep several things in mind. First, the questions are designed to be used just as they are written. If you wish, you may simply read them aloud to the group. Or you may prefer to express them in your own words. However, unnecessary rewording of the questions is not recommended.

Second, the questions are intended to guide the group toward understanding and applying the *main idea* of the passage. The author of the guide has stated his or her view of this central idea in the *purpose* of the study in the leader's notes. You should try to understand how the passage expresses this idea and how the study questions work together to lead the group in that direction.

There may be times when it is appropriate to deviate from the study guide. For example, a question may have already been answered. If so, move on to the next question. Or someone may raise an important question not covered in the guide. Take time to discuss it! The important thing is to use discretion. There may be many routes you can travel to reach the goal of the study. But the easiest route is usually the one the author has suggested.

7. Avoid answering your own questions. If necessary, repeat or rephrase them until they are clearly understood. An eager group quickly becomes passive and silent if they think the leader will do most of the talking.

8. Don't be afraid of silence. People may need time to think about the question before formulating their answers.

9. Don't be content with just one answer. Ask, "What do the rest of you think?" or "Anything else?" until several people have given answers to the question.

10. Acknowledge all contributions. Try to be affirming whenever possible. Never reject an answer. If it is clearly wrong, ask, "Which verse led you to that conclusion?" or again, "What do the rest of you think?"

11. Don't expect every answer to be addressed to you, even though this will probably happen at first. As group members become more at ease, they will begin to truly interact with each other. This is one sign of a healthy discussion.

12. Don't be afraid of controversy. It can be very stimulating. If you don't resolve an issue completely, don't be frustrated. Move on and keep it in mind for later. A subsequent study may solve the problem.

13. Stick to the passage under consideration. It should be the source for answering the questions. Discourage the group from unnecessary cross-referencing. Likewise, stick to the subject and avoid going off on tangents.

14. Periodically summarize what the *group* has said about the passage. This helps to draw together the various ideas mentioned and gives continuity to the study. But don't preach.

15. Conclude your time together with conversational prayer. Be sure to ask God's help to apply those things which you learned in the study.

16. End on time.

Many more suggestions and helps are found in *Leading Bible Discussions* (IVP). Reading and studying through that would be well worth your time.

Components of Small Groups

A healthy small group should do more than study the Bible. There are four components you should consider as you structure your time together.

Nurture. Being a part of a small group should be a nurturing and edifying experience. You should grow in your knowledge and love of God and each other. If we are to properly love God, we must know and keep his commandments (Jn 14:15). That is why Bible study should be a foundational part of your small group. But you can be nurtured by other things as well. You can memorize Scripture, read and discuss a book, or occasionally listen to a tape of a good speaker.

Community. Most people have a need for close friendships. Your small group can be an excellent place to cultivate such relationships. Allow time for informal interaction before and after the study. Have a time of sharing during the meeting. Do fun things together as a group, such as a potluck supper or a picnic. Have someone bring refreshments to the meeting. Be creative!

Worship. A portion of your time together can be spent in worship and prayer. Praise God together for who he is. Thank him for what he has done and is doing in your lives and in the world. Pray for each other's needs. Ask God to help you to apply what you have learned. Sing hymns together.

Mission. Many small groups decide to work together in some form of outreach. This can be a practical way of applying what you have learned. You can host a series of evangelistic discussions for your friends or neighbors. You can visit people at a home for the elderly. Help a widow with cleaning or repair jobs around her home. Such projects can have a transforming influence on your group.

For a detailed discussion of the nature and function of small groups, read *Small Group Leaders' Handbook* or *Good Things Come in Small Groups* (both from IVP).

Study 1. Laying Down the Law. Exodus 20.

Purpose: To discover the setting in which God's law was given and take a preliminary glimpse at the Ten Commandments.

Background. The historical context in which the commandments were given is important. Be prepared to spend several minutes reviewing with your group the background to Exodus 20.

The descendants of Abraham, Isaac and Jacob, who settled in Egypt, had become slaves. Under the leadership of Moses and his brother Aaron and through God's miracles, the children of Israel managed an escape. *Exodus* means "departure" or "exit."

But the book details more than a physical journey; it is a spiritual one as well. Israel's sovereignty as a people is directly related to its dependence on God. Exodus lays the foundation of God's Old Testament revelation about himself: his name, his requirements and how he is to be worshiped. The focal point of this revelation is the giving of the law to Moses at Mount Sinai. The two stone tablets, engraved by no less than God's finger, would later be carried through the desert by the Israelites in the ark of the covenant. All Hebrew law ultimately derives from the commandments.

A brief commentary such as the *New Bible Commentary,* 21st Century Edition, ed. G. J. Wenham et al., (Downers Grove, Ill.: InterVarsity Press, 1994), or the book notes in your study Bible, will provide additional facts about Exodus and the commandments.

Question 3. God points out that he is the one to whom Israel owes its freedom. While the point may seem obvious, we often live in forgetfulness of the grace of God. "The saving action of Yahweh is the prior reality; grace is prior to law" (G. A. Buttrick, ed., *The Interpreter's Dictionary of the Bible* [Nashville: Abingdon, 1962], p. 569).

Question 5. It might be said that God's holiness is the subject of each of these first four commandments. He is the only God; he is beyond idols and images; his very name is holy; we are to keep one day holy in his honor. Group members might also recall Jesus' summary of these commandments: "Love the Lord your God with all your heart and with all your soul and with all your mind" (Mt 22:37). Either way, God's uniqueness and absolute lordship are stressed.

Question 6. Respect for fellow humans is at the center of the final six commands. Each of these directives restrains us from abusing people and their possessions and setting ourselves up as gods. The social fabric is weakened and eventually torn when mutual deference is not shown among us.

Question 7. The fifth commandment, about honoring parents, is the transitional one. It is akin to honoring God (the first four), as well as honoring our neighbor (the final five). The sixth commandment is the first purely social one, and we find it to be the most serious on a descending scale: murder, adultery, stealing, lying and coveting. All sin is serious, of course; the degree is established in the effect upon others.

Question 9. Testing is a frequent theme in Exodus. Children are often "tested" by their parents as well as schoolteachers. The test shows whether a child is listening and learning. The Israelites, as God's children, are "passing the test" by showing an appropriate fear and awe for God's presence and power. Sometimes God must get our attention before we will hear him; the thunder, smoke and lightning accomplish that purpose.

Question 10. God has delivered to his people a code for living before him and in society. It is a grave moment in their history. It is natural and appropriate for the Israelites to show affection and dedication to their Lord through a sacrifice. The ritual also memorializes the moment in a concrete way. Note, as well, that burnt offerings and fellowship offerings are in keeping with the two kinds of commandments (God and society). Fellowship offerings are "better translated as 'communion meals' " (R. Alan Cole, *Exodus* [Downers Grove, Ill.: InterVarsity Press, 1973], p. 163). Finally, sacrifices were meant to atone for sin, which the commandments describe.

Study 2. The One and Only. 1 Kings 18:16-39.

Purpose: To better understand and exalt God as the one and only Lord and identify those concerns which compete for our commitment.

Question 1. Group members need to understand that almost anything can be a "god." Obvious answers are wealth, fame and power, but other possibilities are unlimited.

Question 2. The first commandment provides the basis for the other nine. It offers the most fundamental understanding of God. "Sole allegiance to 'the Lord' lies at the very heart of the covenant relationship. It is the foundation upon which everything else rests" (*New Bible Commentary*, p. 107).

Question 3. Baal was a popular Canaanite God during Elijah's time. "The myths portray Baal as the god of the sky and rain, struggling with Mot, who represents drought" (*The Revell Bible Dictionary,* ed. L. O. Richards [New York: Wynwood, 1990], p. 117).

The story of Elijah and Abah, in which a true believer takes a tough stand for God in an age of spiritual drifting, carries relevance today. Ahab was a strong military leader, but a weak moral guide, always in conflict with God's prophets. Like Ahab, the people nominally honored the Lord, but many were attracted to the pagan deity. Ahab's greeting to Elijah reflects the double-mindedness of Israel, and perhaps an inner realization that the true God is displeased. The king insults the messenger.

Questions 4-5. Elijah is confident enough to take on Baal in Baal territory, and drench an altar he seeks to burn. Those who trust God's sovereignty display such confidence. False gods, and their domains, often provide the setting for God to reveal his power.

Christians need to get out of the sanctuary and demonstrate the power of God in the marketplace, in schools and everywhere else false gods are revered. Elijah chose the one location where divine power would find, and impress, the most people.

Question 6. People tend to be unfaithful to their gods, trying to have it both ways. Elijah challenges his people to have the courage of their convictions and determine once and for all who is really Lord.

The phrase also meaning "to limp" is also used in verse 26 to describe the dance of the Baal prophets. Given Elijah's sarcastic bent, this is probably an intentional pun. And limping, of course, is trying to walk two different ways.

Question 7. Our faith in God is partially built on God's past faithfulness. Old Testament writers frequently referred to "the God of Abraham, Isaac and Israel [Jacob]." We receive inspiration and assurance from what God has done for others, and what he has done for us.

Question 8. Pouring out the water would have been a provocative act before onlookers. In one act Elijah illustrated his faith in God for both fire and rain.

Study 3. Idol Minds. Exodus 32.

Purpose: To define and combat idolatry in the lives of believers.

Question 2. Thomas Watson, the Puritan preacher, said, "In the first commandment worshiping a false god is forbidden. In this, however, the second commandment, worshiping the true God in a false manner is forbidden" (quoted in Stuart Briscoe, *The Ten Commandments: Playing by the Rules* [Wheaton: Shaw, 1993], p. 19). This command is also about trying to control God, whose transcendence cannot be captured in an image or icon. We offer godlike status to some item that is tangible.

Question 4. " 'Zealous' might be a better translation in modern English, since 'jealousy' has acquired an exclusively bad meaning . . . 'Jealousy' does not refer to an emotion so much as to an activity, in this case an activity of violence and vehemence, that springs from the rupture of a personal bond as exclusive as that of the marriage bond. This is not therefore to be seen as intolerance but exclusiveness" (*Exodus,* p. 156). Thus, God is "jealous" as a spouse toward the marriage partner: no rivals will be tolerated. This truth takes in the first two commandments.

Question 5. The phrase "the third and fourth generations" is frequently used in the Old Testament. The Israelites recognized the "domino" effect of sin. In this case, false ideas of worship and the nature of God will particularly mislead and harm our children. Conversely, a home that loves God himself in the right way will reward its descendants.

Question 6. One answer is a void in leadership; the people begin to feel insecure when Moses' absence is prolonged. Also, they wanted a god that was tangible ("gods who will go before us," v. 1).

Question 7. As we've seen, the truth behind this commandment is that God is transcendent; idols rob us of that understanding. As with the gold earrings here, we can only fashion idols from what is ultimately mundane and earthly—and ultimately unfulfilling. It is not surprising that gold, of some sort, would become the first substitute for God.

Question 8. The idol led the Israelites into feasting and revelry (apparently orgies). The true God elevates our stature; false ones enhance our sinfulness.

Question 9. Moses indicates his concern for the godly reputation of his people in Exodus 33:16. From Abraham's covenant the Israelites were to represent and illuminate God in the world. In the same way Christians must not sink to the world's standards. Mundane idolatry and "revelry" of any kind send a message about ourselves and the God we represent.

Question 10. Readers of the Old Testament naturally seek explanations of violent passages such as this one. God is concerned for keeping his people pure from the spread of outright disobedience and rebellionism such as this. In general, idolatry is among the most destructive of sins. To spread a diminished, mundane idea of God is to poison the cultural air we breathe. To attempt to control God through idols is also a path to devastation. The Israelites, for example, finally found themselves sacrificing children to a god called Molech (see Lev 18:21; 20:3-5; Jer 32:35). As God is transcendent, it is imperative to keep our doctrine and worship of him pure. Also see Walter C. Kaiser, *Hard Sayings of the Old Testament* (Downers Grove, Ill.: InterVarsity Press, 1988), pp. 106-9.

Study 4. Respect for the Name. Psalm 96.

Purpose: To discover the holiness of God's name and be inspired to use it respectfully.

Question 2. Names are extremely important throughout Scripture. Abraham, Peter and Paul all bear changed names to reflect changed identities. "In biblical times the name was considered an extension or expression of the person himself" (*Revell Bible Dictionary*, p. 722). The name of God (YHWH) was considered far more sacred than today, and priests actually spoke it only once per year (on the Day of Atonement). Also, his continuing presence and power were considered absolute, and to use his name casually was a blatant denial of that reality.

Question 3. The first commandment deals with worshiping God only. "Whereas the second commandment prohibits visual representations of God, the third focuses on verbal representations" (*New Bible Commentary*, p. 107). It concerns, again, an attempt to control God, this time by the use of his name.

Question 5. The *New Bible Commentary* entitles this psalm, "The only God and his gospel." The verses call on God's people to praise his name and to invite the nations to do so. Even the natural world is called upon to issue praise to its Creator. The psalm ends in an evocation of God's future judgement in righteousness and truth.

Question 7. Of course we are praising God by praising his name. But to praise his name means to praise what we know of God. His name takes in his reputation, tradition and expression in the world (just as one's family name has a reputation and a tradition).

Question 10. An offering, of course, is not limited to a church budget contribution. It can be many things. The act of sacrifice heightens our awareness of God being more than worthy of our gift and of the ultimate sacrifice he made for us. Whenever we make any kind of offering, we should do so in his name, reflecting prayerfully on it.

Study 5. Respect for Sabbath Rest. Psalm 16.

Purpose: To consider God's institution of a cycle of work and rest, and the observance of the Sabbath in God's honor.

Question 2. This commandment affirms that we are created in the image of God. He observed the seven day work/rest cycle, and ordains that we do so. Amidst the stern demands of the Ten Commandments, this directive provides a reminder that the commandments serve to protect us. As we ignore the command to rest, it can be no coincidence that problems with stress and burnout are rampant in our society.

Question 4. The psalmist finds delight in the Lord (v. 2), in God's people (v. 3) and in God's teaching (v. 7). Appropriately, we might find all three as we gather congregationally.

Question 5. "To say 'The Lord is . . . my cup' is to affirm that in sorrow or joy he is the overriding reality" (*New Bible Commentary,* p. 495). The psalmist realizes that God is sovereign over every aspect of his life, and this brings peace and security.

Question 7. Maintaining an ongoing sense of God's presence is a vital Christian discipline. Believers can do a number of practical things to enhance this attitude, such as placing scriptural reminders on the refrigerator or the car's dashboard, keeping Christian music playing in the background or memorizing a verse a week. Perhaps the most effective strategy is to maintain a regular daily quiet time with God.

Question 12. You might divide into pairs and pray for each other's current concerns to close the meeting.

Study 6. Respect for Parents. Ruth 1:1-18.

Purpose: To discover the value of honoring our parents and commit ourselves to doing so.

Question 2. One possibility is that obedience to parents is the first issue a person faces in his or her lifespan. So it would precede the other five "social" commandments for chronological reasons. But there is at least one other reason. "The obligations of son [or daughter] to parents is a deeply religious one and comes to be used to describe the relation between Israel and her God (Jer. 31:30; Hos. 11:1). This commandment thus provides a good 'bridge' between the two parts of the Ten Commandments" (*The Interpreter's Dictionary of the Bible,* pp. 569-70). It is a "segue" commandment, in other words.

Question 3. This commandment is not presented as God's offer of a deal. It is more like a law of common sense. Those who respect and revere the elderly are enhancing the environment for their own retirement. Our children are likely to treat us with the same respect, after they are grown, that they see us give to their grandparents. Our motives are not simply philanthropic; we have a real need for the accumulated wisdom of the previous generation.

Question 5. Like any good parent (and remember that Naomi has had, and lost, two sons), Naomi puts the children's welfare before her own. The prospects of remarriage would be much better for the young women in their own country. Given the difficulties and dangers of Naomi's journey, and the fact that the two girls are the last of her family, she is making a considerable sacrifice. Clearly Naomi is a "parent" worthy of honor.

Question 6. Surviving a husband and outliving her own children, Naomi understandably feels there has been little providence for her. "The Lord's hand has gone out against me!" would be a very human response. Your group members should understand that this is another motive for honoring our parents: the years can bring bitterness, and our forebears are worthy of the loving care that can take the sting out. They have done so for us often enough. **Question 7.** She parts ways with her sister-in-law, a more logical companion than her older, foreign mother-in-law. She leaves her homeland and casts her uncertain lot in a strange country. She chooses the dangers of travel. Ruth and Naomi are dual models of the choice of wisdom over expedience.

Question 11. Creative ways to honor our elders are not difficult to find. A good start might be a greeting card with a warm, personal note of gratitude on a special day—or a non-special one. The best expression of love is often time, and we can find extra time to spend with parents or "significant elders." We need to reflect on the sacrifices made for us by those who have gone before, and verbalize our appreciation, while there is still time.

Study 7. Respect for Life. 1 Samuel 24.

Purpose: To discover the godly value of life and commit ourselves to respecting it however possible.

Question 2. The fewer the words, the more serious the tone communicated. These acts are strictly forbidden, in many cases bringing the death penalty in ancient Israel. This is a good place to note, however, that the Hebrew idea of murder is differentiated from the killing involved in capital punishment or war (see *Exodus,* pp. 159-60). Arguments against those concepts must be made from the New Testament, of course.

Question 3. Saul became Israel's first king (1 Sam 10). Despite his considerable gifts and a strong beginning, his reign quickly deteriorated. He never grasped that God was still the nation's ultimate ruler. His subjects began to transfer their affections to the young hero David, who had defeated the giant Goliath and had already been anointed as Saul's successor (1 Sam 16). Saul, quite naturally, felt threatened by his perceived usurper. The palace divided into political factions. As this passage begins, David has been forced to flee from the murderous king.

In verse 4 note how the sycophantic supporters take God's words out of context to justify a wrong and cowardly act.

Question 6. Note that David could flee quietly and still have claimed the moral high ground. But he clearly risks his life in calling Saul out of the cave, for the king has previously given no evidence of a merciful spirit. However, more than simply refusing to retaliate, David turns away wrath with a gentle word (as well as some mild confrontation, v. 12).

Question 9. Throughout our long and complex biblical portrait of David, one attribute is consistent: his way with words! Having shown the piece of Saul's robe, he has positioned the king to appear cowardly if he murders

David. Now he compares his vulnerability before the king to that of "a dead dog" or "a flea." And, stating the decision in terms of God's vindication, the entire confrontation takes on a new appearance for Saul.

Question 10. He spares David, and requests an oath that his descendants will receive the same mercy. One of the worst aspects of evildoing is the cycle of vengeance that begins. Saul realizes he can't thwart David's ascent, which is clearly God's will. The best he can do is to prevent the murderous cycle.

Question 11. David's kingship may be a foregone conclusion, but Saul has guaranteed his future safety, and that of his descendants, from David's hand. As for David, he has set the tone for a wise and just rule. He has refused to secure his fate using treachery. Note also that David affects those around him: he refuses to let his men kill Saul (v. 7).

Study 8. Respect for Marriage. 2 Samuel 11.

Purpose: To discover the danger of adultery and resolve to avoid temptation.

Question 1. A related phenomenon is the failure of marriages. Studies show that 50% of all new marriages will end in divorce; 70% of all second marriages and 82% of third attempts are doomed to failure. The median age for divorce is now 28. Of course, the divorce and adultery rates mutually affect each other.

Question 2. The first four commandments concern respect for and faithfulness to God. Marriage, to a lesser extent, is holy and the spouse merits the same kind of priority, faithfulness and respect on a human scale. The fifth commandment can also be called a "family commandment."

Question 3. David sends someone "to find out about her" (v. 3). This seemingly small step makes the later poor decisions possible. It also seems that David has time on his hands, during a period when he might have been with his troops in the line of battle. Instead, he has placed himself in the line of temptation.

Question 4. The trajectory of sin leads from adultery to furtive manipulation. David attempts to cover his sin by insuring that Bathsheba's husband sleeps with her close in proximity to her conception. He knows that the soldiers have taken an oath to abstain from sexual relations (1 Sam 21:4-5). Note Uriah's loyalty to his oath in sleeping in the doorway, which foils David's plan. "Wash your feet" was a colloquial expression for "spend time at home."

Question 6. David gives in to temptation, then tries to cover his sin with more sin. Uriah's incorruptibility contributes to David's growing desperation, and he chooses a sin far worse than anything before it. You might briefly compare this spiral of corruption to James 1:14-15. Note David's coldest touch: having Uriah deliver his own death warrant (v. 14).

Question 9. David's coded message to Joab is, of course, cold-hearted. Then he makes Bathsheba his wife, though she mourns the husband he has slain. It is clear that David has lost his "moral compass." David will feel no remorse until Nathan's clarifying confrontation in the next chapter.

The second part of the question offers an opportunity for a sobering contrast of David the adulterous king with the David of the preceding study (1 Sam 24), a young man of humility whose actions seemed dictated by conscience. While it is impossible to read David's heart with precision, we can observe that he is now a man of power. Perhaps this access to power and luxury has (at least temporarily) dulled David's conscience. It may be that the massive proportions of his sin have blinded him to its gravity. Or David may have been suppressing his guilt.

Question 10. His sins include coveting, murder, adultery and, arguably, lying (given his deception of Uriah). This would total four of the six "social" commandments.

Study 9. Respect for Property. Acts 4:32—5:11.

Purpose: To understand the varieties of stealing and build respect for the property of others.

Question 2. The study's introduction provides an illustration that might hit a nerve or two. Encourage group members to think of subtle instances of taking what isn't one's own. For example, ignoring the right-of-way at a traffic intersection, pirating cable television, taking office supplies home from work or even stealing *time* through tardiness.

Question 3. Luke tells us that "the outpouring of God's Spirit here leads not only to miracles and inspired verbal witness but also to actively caring for one another and sharing possessions" (Craig S. Keener, *The IVP Bible Background Commentary: New Testament* [Downers Grove: InterVarsity Press, 1993], p. 334). As unity and fellowship are deepened, a spirit of generosity grows—quite the opposite of what the commandment prohibits.

Question 4. Since greed is so prevalent in the world, sincere generosity attracts attention.

Question 6. Personal ownership is in no way negated. The Christians in Acts retain their possessions, but simply share them willingly.

Question 7. Certainly most prominent is the sin of lying. As we study the commandments, we notice that the major sins are entangled with each other. It is difficult to break one commandment without breaking others.

Question 8. Peter casts the situation in the light of, respectively, the Spirit, Satan and God. Those who live in obedience are able to maintain a spiritual perspective.

Question 9. This may be the most troubling question for group members. It is important to consider the context: the church, in Acts, is in its infancy. The future of Christianity rests with the "charter members." Maintaining purity is absolutely essential. The weed of sin is extracted before it can spread, and a solemn message is communicated.

Study 10. Respect for the Truth. Proverbs 12.

Purpose: To discover the damage of dishonesty and to seek personal integrity.

Question 2. Lying cuts right to Satan's chief concern: the truth and how to separate humanity from it. Dishonesty alienates us from God and from each other.

Question 3. The commandments are arranged, in roughly descending order of severity, from our regard for God, to our treatment of God, to our behavior among ourselves, to our words and thoughts. The last two commandments—concerning lying and coveting—fall in this final category. This is not to suggest that lying is a sin of low magnitude (as we've seen, it is Satan's chosen strategy). But it might, in many situations, be less damaging in its effect on others than killing, adultery and stealing. Coveting, in turn, might never affect another person.

Question 7. Our words impact those around us and determine how we are received in the world, among other things. One who uses speech positively and productively creates a beneficial environment.

The second part of the question considers the idea that words and work (the two themes of this section of the Proverbs) are inextricably mingled. The godly person will speak and act in truth.

Question 8. The real concern of the writer is not simply truth as an abstract consideration; but rather, our destruction of others and ourselves through our words. Lying and ill-considered statements both come from a heart out of synch with God's ways.

Concerning the second part of the question, the short answer is yes. One can indeed speak the truth recklessly. Paul tells us to speak the truth in love (Eph 4:15). Some use the truth as a weapon. Again, biblical writers do not discuss truth in the abstract; the important thing is always our standing with God and each other.

Study 11. The Value of Contentment. 1 Timothy 6:3-10.
Purpose: To gain an understanding of the nature and effect of coveting and to strive for "godliness with contentment."
Question 1. An accurate understanding of the word *covet* is essential for this study. The Hebrew word is *desire,* which is not sin in itself; the key distinction is that when something owned by someone else is the object, desiring becomes coveting.
Question 2. Coveting is a "gateway sin" which leads to many other commandment violations. Obedience to this final Word serves as "preventive maintenance" for others. See also the note for study 10, question 3.
Question 3. One possibility: A "thought crime" needs to be "fleshed out" for the hearers. Also, the examples demonstrate how broad are the implications to this commandment.
Question 5. Paul deals frequently in his letter with teachers of heresy. Some of these teachers have taken the classic teaching that those who follow God's law tend to prosper and distorted it into religion with a profit motive. Wealth is a reasonable, possible by-product of godliness, not the incentive for it.
Question 6. Paul uses financial metaphors to make his own point. In verse 5 the profiteers are "robbed" of the truth; in verse 6 it is godliness, not finance, which is "gain." Paul thus underlines the distinctions between spiritual and monetary motives.
Question 7. Contentment is a by-product of godliness. Becoming godly nurtures within us God's perspective, which is that we have, in him, everything we need. This liberation from material longing is indeed great gain.
Question 8. Christians can be content, and happy, while still having ambitions for other reasonable goals. The real question is whether or not God is first in our hearts, and whether godliness defines and directs the ambitions.
Question 11. The answer: any or all of the other nine. See the note for question 2.

Study 12. The Law of Grace. Romans 3:9-31.
Purpose: To consider the relationship between law and grace, and to deepen our security in Christ's redeeming grace.
General Note. For some Christians, this study will seem basic; for newer believers, it will be complex. Be sure to thoroughly review Romans 3 (and, for context, Romans 2) before the study. Be ready to explain terms like "atonement," "grace" and "justification."

Question 2. Two possibilities: Paul's assertion that righteousness is not possible through the law and his statement that Gentiles and Jews "alike are all under sin."

Question 4. The power of sin extends to all humanity. We are "under sin" in the sense that through our human abilities we cannot avoid sin's daily damage. By "the law" Jews understand that there are specific works found in God's law (the Old Testament Scriptures) that are requirements for pleasing God. Apart from Christ, all people are subject to the cycle of sin's power and the law's requirements.

Question 6. *Righteousness* refers to an individual's conformity with God's laws. *Justification* is meeting that standard and being declared innocent. *Grace* is God's generous action to us above and beyond what justice would require. *Redemption* is the payment of a required price to free or obtain something.

Question 9. A Jewish reader of this letter might be proud of his faithfulness to the law. Paul, through his argument, shows the folly of boasting when human righteousness (apart from grace) is impossible.

Question 10. Before, attempting to live by the law seemed futile, but with the perspective of grace we can obey God's commandments to uphold the law, confident he has already accepted us. Again, Jesus said he came "not to abolish [the Law or Prophets] but to fulfill them" (Mt 5:17).

Rob Suggs is a freelance writer, illustrator and cartoonist. He is also the author of the LifeGuide® Bible Study Christian Community *and several humor books. He lives with his wife and two children in Atlanta, Georgia.*

What Should We Study Next?

A good place to start your study of Scripture would be with a book study. Many groups begin with a Gospel such as *Mark* (22 studies by James Hoover) or *John* (26 studies by Douglas Connelly). These guides are divided into two parts so that if 22 or 26 weeks seems like too much to do at once, the group can feel free to do half and take a break with another topic. Later you might want to come back to it. You might prefer to try a shorter letter. *Philippians* (9 studies by Donald Baker), *Ephesians* (13 studies by Andrew T. and Phyllis J. Le Peau) and *1 & 2 Timothy and Titus* (12 studies by Pete Sommer) are good options. If you want to vary your reading with an Old Testament book, consider *Ecclesiastes* (12 studies by Bill and Teresa Syrios) for a challenging and exciting study.

There are a number of interesting topical LifeGuide studies as well. Here are some options for filling three or four quarters of a year:

Basic Discipleship
Christian Beliefs, 12 studies by Stephen D. Eyre
Christian Character, 12 studies by Andrea Sterk & Peter Scazzero
Christian Disciplines, 12 studies by Andrea Sterk & Peter Scazzero
Evangelism, 12 studies by Rebecca Pippert & Ruth Siemens

Spiritual Growth
Fruit of the Spirit, 9 studies by Hazel Offner
Faith, 9 studies by Dale & Sandy Larsen
Hope, 9 studies by Jack Kuhatschek
Love, 9 studies by Phyllis J. Le Peau

Character Studies
New Testament Characters, 12 studies by Carolyn Nystrom
Old Testament Characters, 12 studies by Peter Scazzero
Old Testament Kings, 12 studies by Carolyn Nystrom
Women of the Old Testament, 12 studies by Gladys Hunt

The Trinity
Meeting God, 12 studies by J. I. Packer
Meeting Jesus, 13 studies by Leighton Ford
Meeting the Spirit, 12 studies by Douglas Connelly